THE PLEDGE
OF ALLEGIANCE

SCHOLASTIC INC. Cartwheel BOOKS®

New York   Toronto   London   Auckland   Sydney   Mexico City   New Delhi   Hong Kong

Photography credits for *The Pledge of Allegiance*:
Cover: John Fleck/Stone; Back Cover: Art Montes De Oca/FPG; page 3: Chip Henderson/Stone;
page 4: SuperStock; page 5, top left: Chromosohn/Photo Researchers, right: Philip Spears/FPG, bottom left: Steve Skjold/PhotoEdit;
page 6, top left: Toyohiro Yamada/FPG, top right: Dennis Flaherty/Photo Researchers, bottom right: FPG, bottom left: SuperStock;
page 7: Harvey Lloyd/FPG; page 8: Paul Sakuma/AP Wide World Photo; page 9: Owen Franken/Corbis; page 10: NASA/AP Wide World Photo;
page 11, top left: Jerry Alexander/Stone, right: Peter Gridley/FPG, bottom left: SuperStock; page 12: PhotoDisc; page 13: Robert W. Ginn/PhotoEdit;
pages 14-15: Art Montes De Oca/FPG; page 16, left: SuperStock; pages 16-17: Arthur Tilley/FPG; page 18, background: David Young Wolff/PhotoEdit,
top left: Myrleen Ferguson Cate/PhotoEdit, right: Philip Spears/FPG, bottom left: Michelle & Tom Grimm/Stone; page 19: Art Montes De Oca/FPG;
page 20, left: Reza Estakhrian/Stone; pages 20-21: SuperStock; page 22: FPG; page 23: Michael Newman/PhotoEdit; page 24: FPG.

ISBN 0-439-21672-9

Copyright © 2000 by Scholastic Inc.
All rights reserved.   Published by Scholastic Inc.
SCHOLASTIC, CARTWHEEL BOOKS and associated logos are trademarks and/or
registered trademarks of Scholastic Inc.

10 9 8 7 6 5 4   00 01 02 03 04

Printed in the U.S.A.   08
First printing, September 2000

I pledge allegiance

to the flag

of the United States of America

and to the Republic

for which it stands,

one Nation

under God,

indivisible,

with liberty

and justice

for all.

I pledge allegiance
to the flag
of the United States of America
and to the Republic
for which it stands,
one Nation
under God,
indivisible,
with liberty
and justice
for all.